E.M. UHLENBECK
Bio-bibliographical notice

CENTRE INTERNATIONAL DE DIALECTOLOGIE GÉNÉRALE

BIOBIBLIOGRAPHIES ET EXPOSÉS

N.S. 5

E.M. UHLENBECK

Bio-bibliographical notice

by M. JANSE and P. SWIGGERS

followed by Prof. UHLENBECK's address:

"Javanese Linguistics, A Retrospect and Some Prospects"

LEUVEN

CENTRE INTERNATIONAL DE DIALECTOLOGIE GÉNÉRALE

Blijde-Inkomststraat 21

1996

ISBN 2-87723-309-x (Peeters France)
ISBN 90-6831-884-5 (Peeters Leuven)
D. 1996/0602/108

FOREWORD

The work of E.M. Uhlenbeck falls within the best tradition of European structuralist linguistics, and exemplifies very accurately what is covered, in principle, by the term "general linguistics". Throughout his career Uhlenbeck has been interested in the fundamental problems of general linguistics, such as the relation between form and meaning, the status of the word, the definition of linguistic units in general, the specificity (and autonomy) of linguistics, the relationship between language use and language description. Uhlenbeck's general linguistics is grounded in thorough empirical work, on both European and non-European languages. Among the latter, Javanese has been his principal field of investigation. For more than half a century Uhlenbeck has been one of the world's leading specialists on this language, which he has studied in great detail, from both a synchronic and diachronic point of view, combining linguistic description with extensive philological documentation.

The "encounter" with Javanese was a turning point in Uhlenbeck's intellectual development: it made him aware that linguistic description must be based on objective grounds, not on traditional frameworks set up for a particular type of languages. Uhlenbeck's linguistic ideas took shape at a period when linguistic theorizing was still wrestling with the systematization of grammar at the level of morphology; very soon Uhlenbeck — who had tackled intricate issues such as reduplication and the status of word classes in Javanese — realized that the distributional treatment of morphology fell short of integrating meaning in the description. Also, he recognized that linguistic description cannot dispense with the (admittedly problematic) concept of "word": the word is an "inter-level" unit of language in that it is involved in morphophonology, in morphology and in syntax. Words are units in which the essential properties of language show up: patterning (according to positive and negative rules), proportionality and productivity. From this results the complexity of morphological description, which must contain categories, lists of forms, types of rules, and (general as well as specific) statements on distribution and/or aspects of meaning.

His studies of Javanese morphology brought Uhlenbeck to lay the foundations of a theory of general linguistics, which is indebted to various brands of European structuralism, to American structuralism, but most specifically to the views of A. Reichling and H.J. Pos. This resulted in a comprehensive view of language structure and language description, which stressed the productivity and potentiality of language, without, however, accepting the basic assumptions of generative grammar. From his early criticisms of generative linguistics on Uhlenbeck has opposed the distinction between competence and performance, the distinction between surface and deep structure, the idea of a separate semantic structure, and the modularity of grammar. In addition he has been a harsh critic of the type of argumentation found in generative writings.

In his linguistic theory Uhlenbeck has made the word and the sentence the two central units of linguistic structure. The word is an interlevel unit between morpho(phono)logy and syntax, and the sentence is a structured combination of words. In this combination two components interfere: the intonational and the phatic component. In his publications on syntax Uhlenbeck has repeatedly stressed that syntax cannot be restricted to the study of word-grouping and the analysis of relations holding between units in a formal representation. Syntax is basically a matter of expressing complex information through a linguistic structure, the use and interpretation of which also involve extralinguistic information. As such, Uhlenbeck has challenged the generative approach, in making syntax instrumental in relation to word-meaning.

Uhlenbeck's view of language can be characterized as "functional" and "realist": his central concern is with what language structures achieve, how language functions in communication, and how humans living in society use linguistic structures.

M. Janse – P. Swiggers
Linguistic Bibliography / University of Ghent –
Belgian National Science Foundation

E.M. Uhlenbeck:
Bio-bibliographical notice

by

M. JANSE AND P. SWIGGERS

E.M. UHLENBECK: BIOGRAPHICAL NOTICE

Eugenius Marius ("Bob") Uhlenbeck was born on August 9, 1913 in The Hague. After attending school at the Gymnasium Haganum, he enrolled in 1932 at the University of Leiden, for the study of Indology, and at the University of Utrecht, for the study of Indonesian Law. After having graduated in 1937 from both universities he fulfilled his military service in the Netherlands and then left for Indonesia ("the Dutch Indies") to work for the government at Balai Pustaka (Bureau for Popular Literature) in Jakarta (Batavia) as a specialist of Javanese language and literature.

The years at Balai Pustaka proved to be crucial in Uhlenbeck's development as a scholar of Javanese and as a general linguist. Surrounded with native speakers of Javanese he acquired a thorough command of the language: "Six days a week, seven hours per day of either reading, speaking or listening to Javanese prepared me for the study of Javanese in an unparalleled way"[1]. The director of Balai Pustaka, K.A.H. Hidding, introduced him to the work of the Dutch philosopher and linguist Hendrik J. Pos (1898-1955), which gave Uhlenbeck a first entry in general linguistics. Uhlenbeck soon immersed himself in the study of the works of Ferdinand de Saussure (1857-1913), Edward Sapir (1884-1939), Leonard Bloomfield (1887-1949) and Karl Bühler (1879-1963), and he also read carefully the writings of Hermann Paul (1846-1921), Wilhelm Wundt (1832-1920) and Georg von der Gabelentz (1840-1933).

In 1941 Uhlenbeck became acquainted, through the reading of Nicolaas van Wijk's (1880-1941) *Phonologie*[2], with the writings of the Prague School; he then took up the study of the works of Vilém Mathesius (1882-1945), Nikolaj Trubeckoj (1890-1938) and Roman Jakobson (1896-1982). Uhlenbeck realized that an important revolution was taking place in linguistics: the historical-comparative paradigm, which had been dominant for a century, was being replaced by a synchronic linguistics focusing on the systemic nature of language(s). Faced with this emerging paradigm of "immanent" language description and confronted with the task of analysing Javanese Uhlenbeck became suspicious of the framework of traditional grammar, conceived for languages like Latin

---

[1] E.M. Uhlenbeck, *Javanese Linguistics, A Retrospect and Some Prospects* (Dordrecht, 1983), 10 [see *infra*, p. 37].

[2] N. van Wijk, *Phonologie: een hoofdstuk uit de structurele taalwetenschap* (Den Haag, 1939); see E.M. Uhlenbeck, "De betekenis van de phonologie", *Tijdschrift van het Koninklijk Bataviaasch Genootschap van Kunsten en Wetenschappen* 82 (1948), 312-329 and his review article of *L'école de Prague aujourd'hui* (Prague, 1964), *Lingua* 17 (1967), 358-365.

and Greek[3]. As a result he avoided using traditional syntactic criteria for distinguishing between basic sentence types, but based his description of Javanese sentence structure on intonation[4].

Under the Japanese occupation of Indonesia Uhlenbeck was a prisoner of war for three years. After the war he became lecturer in General and Indonesian Linguistics at the University of Indonesia in Jakarta, where he taught from 1946 till 1948. In these years he prepared his Ph.D. dissertation under the supervision of his Leiden professor Cornelis C. Berg (1900-1990); as his subject he chose the phonology and morphology of Javanese. The thesis, defended in 1949[5], combines insights from Prague structuralism (such as the distinction between "centre" and "periphery"), with distributional analysis as well as with theoretical views developed by Uhlenbeck (such as the distinction between exceptionless rules and statistical rules allowing for exceptions).

In 1949 Uhlenbeck returned to the Netherlands. He joined the editorial board of the *Bijdragen tot de Taal-, Land- en Volkenkunde*, revived its companion series *Verhandelingen en Werken*, and took the initiative of launching two new series, the *Bibliographical Series* and the *Translation Series*. In 1950 he was elected as a member of the board of the Royal Institute of Linguistics and Anthropology (*Koninklijk Instituut voor Taal-, Land- en Volkenkunde*)[6]. The same year Uhlenbeck took over Berg's chair of Javanese language and literature at the University of Leiden[7]. His teaching forced him to develop a coherent and comprehensive theory of morphology, along the lines followed for the description of phonological structures. In developing his theory of morphology

---

[3] E.M. Uhlenbeck, "Traditionele zinsontleding en syntaxis", *Levende Talen* 193 (1958), 18-30; see also: "De studie der zgn. exotische talen in verband met de algemene taalwetenschap", *Museum* 61 (1956), 65-80 (translation: "The Study of the So-Called Exotic Languages and General Linguistics", *Lingua* 9 [1960], 417-434).

[4] See his: *Beknopte Javaansche grammatica*, Batavia, 1941; "Het onderzoek der intonatie-verschijnselen", *Handelingen van het vierentwintigste Nederlands Filologencongres (Amsterdam, 5-6 april 1956)*, 77-78.

[5] It was published under the title: *De structuur van het Javaanse morpheem*, Bandoeng, 1949; see also the condensed English version: "The Structure of the Javanese Morpheme", *Lingua* 2 (1950), 239-270.

[6] Uhlenbeck managed to secure the existence of the internationally renowned Institute in the late fifties; it was transferred from The Hague to Leiden in 1967. Uhlenbeck was President of the Institute between 1962 and 1965. See E.M. Uhlenbeck, "Perspectief der Nederlandse Oriëntalistiek", *Bijdragen tot de Taal-, Land- en Volkenkunde* 123 (1967), 205-216.

[7] In the 1950s Uhlenbeck published extensively on Javanese morphology; see his articles "The Study of Word Classes in Javanese", *Lingua* 3 (1953), 322-354; "Woordverdubbeling in het Javaans", *Bijdragen tot de Taal-, Land- en Volkenkunde* 109 (1953), 52-61; "De systematiek der Javaanse telwoorden", *Bijdragen tot de Taal-, Land- en Volkenkunde* 109 (1953), 342-375; "Verdubbelingsprocédé's bij het Javaanse werkwoord", *Bijdragen tot de Taal-, Land- en Volkenkunde* 110 (1954), 369-387; "Over woordvorming

Uhlenbeck took inspiration from the work of Anton Reichling (1898-1986), who had posited the word as the central unit of language use and language analysis, and had stressed the difference in status between the word and the morpheme[8]. In 1951 Uhlenbeck joined Reichling and Anton Willem de Groot (1892-1963) on the editorial board of *Lingua*, the Dutch international journal of general linguistics founded in 1948[9].

It was in *Lingua* that Uhlenbeck published his first theoretical reflections on morphology, based on his study of descriptive issues in Javanese[10]. Over three decades Uhlenbeck published extensively on Javanese morphology; in 1978 the results of these studies were synthesized in a comprehensive volume[11].

In developing a theory of morphology — in which the word plays a central role, and in which morphemes are taken as markers or exponents dependent upon the word category in which they appear — Uhlenbeck found inspiration in the theoretical principles of the Prague School. Within European structuralism the notions of potentiality and productivity had been proposed by Mathesius and S. Karcevskij[12], and Uhlenbeck refined both concepts[13], applying them to morphological processes[14].

---

in het Javaans", *Bijdragen tot de Taal-, Land- en Volkenkunde* 111 (1955), 286-307; "Verb Structure in Javanese", in M. Halle - H.G. Lunt - H. McLean - C.H. van Schooneveld (eds.), *For Roman Jakobson. Essays on the occasion of his sixtieth birthday* (The Hague, 1956), 567-573; "Die mit javanisch *rasa* morphologisch zusammenhängenden Wörter. Ein Beitrag zur javanischen Lexikologie", *Oriens Extremus* 6 (1959), 104-115.

[8] See A. Reichling, *Het woord: een studie omtrent de grondslag van taal en taalgebruik*, Zwolle, 1935; see E.M. Uhlenbeck's obituary "Anton Reichling: Nijmegen 9 juli 1898 - Amsterdam 25 mei 1986", *Jaarboek van de Maatschappij der Nederlandse Letterkunde te Leiden 1986-1987* (1988), 110-120.

[9] Uhlenbeck remained on the editorial board of *Lingua* until 1984.

[10] See the articles referred to in notes 5 and 7; see also "Limitations of Morphological Processes. Some preliminary remarks", *Lingua* 11 [= Festschrift A.W. de Groot] (1962), 426-432.

[11] E.M. Uhlenbeck, *Studies in Javanese Morphology* (The Hague, 1978).

[12] See V. Mathesius, "O potenciálnosti jevů jazykových", *Věstnik Královské české společnosti nauk* 2 (1911), 1-24 [Translated as: "On the Potentiality of the Phenomena of Language", in J. Vachek ed., *A Prague School Reader in Linguistics* (Bloomington, 1964), 1-32]; S. Karcevskij, "Autour d'un problème de morphologie", *Annales Academiae Scientiarum Fennicae* series B 27 (1932), 84-91.

[13] See E.M. Uhlenbeck, "The Concepts of Productivity and Potentiality in Morphological Description and their Psycholinguistic Reality", in G. Drachman (ed.), *Akten der 3. Salzburger Jahrestagung für Linguistik (Psycholinguistik) 1976* (Salzburg, 1977), 379-392; "Productivity and Creativity, Some Remarks on the Dynamic Aspects of Language", in W. Dietrich - H. Geckeler - B. Schlieben-Lange - J. Trabant - H. Weydt (eds.), *Logos Semantikos. Studia Linguistica in Honorem Eugenio Coseriu 1921-1981* (Berlin - New York - Madrid, 1981), vol. III, 165-174; "General Linguistics and the Study of Morphological Processes", *Oceanic Linguistics* 31 (1992), 1-11.

[14] Uhlenbeck distinguishes four general types of morphological processes: (1) addition of material to the radical (prefixation, infixation, suffixation or any combination of

Methodological reflection on his analysis of Javanese brought Uhlenbeck to a theory of general linguistics firmly rooted in the tradition of
European structuralism, enriched with insights from the philosophy and
psychology of language. In 1958 Uhlenbeck became Professor of General
Linguistics at the University of Leiden[15]. He was soon confronted with
the rise of transformational-generative linguistics, and was one of the
first European linguists to react critically. Uhlenbeck opposed Chomsky's conception of an autonomous syntax, detached from a semantic
component — a heritage of Neo-Bloomfieldian linguistics[16] — and he
criticized generative linguists for their candid adoption of the categories
of traditional grammar[17].

As a teacher and practitioner of general linguistics Uhlenbeck saw the
need of working out a viable alternative to transformational grammar
which could serve as a general introduction to linguistic theory. His

---

these three); (2) modification of the radical (both of segments and suprasegments);
(3) reduplication; (4) compounding or the combination of two or more radicals. See
"Morphonology and Morphology: Two Systematic Aspects of Word Structure", in
W. Winter (ed.), *On Languages and Language. The Presidential Addresses of the 1991
Meeting of the Societas Linguistica Europaea* (Berlin - New York, 1995), 257-266 (p. 262-
263); "Clitics, Morphemes, and Words: Their Structural Differences", in W. Bahner -
J. Schildt - D. Viehweger (eds.), *Proceedings of the 14th International Congress of
Linguists, Berlin/GDR, August 10 - August 15, 1987* (Berlin, 1990), 637-641 (p. 638).

[15] Uhlenbeck published a number of introductions to the study of language and to
structural linguistics: "Taalwetenschap", in E.J. Dijksterhuis ed., *Scientia. Handboek
voor wetenschap, kunst en religie* (Zeist, 1956) I, 258-275; *Taalwetenschap, een eerste
inleiding* (The Hague, 1959; ninth edition in 1980); "Structurele Taalwetenschap", in
F. Balk-Smit Duyzentkunst *et al.*, *Controversen in de taal- en literatuurwetenschap*
(Wassenaar, 1974), 137-146; *Taal en Taalwetenschap* (Leiden, 1976); *Het wonder van
de natuurlijke taal* (Haarlem, 1980).

[16] E.M. Uhlenbeck, "Linguistics in America 1924-1974. A Detached View", in
H.M. Hoenigswald (ed.), *The European Background of American Linguistics. Papers of
the Third Golden Anniversary Symposium of the Linguistic Society of America, December
27, 1974* (Dordrecht, 1979), 121-144, 153-157; see already his review of C. Mohrmann -
A. Sommerfelt - J. Whatmough (eds.), *Trends in European and American Linguistics
1930-1960* and C. Mohrmann - F. Norman - A. Sommerfelt (eds.), *Trends in Modern
Linguistics*, in *Romance Philology* 19 (1965), 353-360.

[17] For Uhlenbeck's critical reflections on transformational-generative grammar, see:
"An Appraisal of Transformation Theory", *Lingua* 12 (1963), 1-18; "Some Further
Remarks on Transformational Grammar", *Lingua* 17 (1967), 263-316; "On the Notion
of 'Completely Novel Sentences'", *Cahiers Ferdinand de Saussure* 26 (1969), 179-
186; "Transformational-Generative Grammar and the Teaching of Foreign Languages:
A Critical Appraisal", in A.J. van Essen - J.P. Menting (eds.), *The Context of Foreign-
Language Learning* (Assen, 1975), 152-158. Most of these critical assessments are
collected in Uhlenbeck's *Critical Comments on Transformational-Generative Grammar
1962-1972* (The Hague, 1973). For a subsequently published appraisal, see Uhlenbeck's
"Nederlandse voorlichting over generatieve grammatica", *Forum der Letteren* 18 (1977),
167-210.

theorizing was based, as previously in his career, on empirical data, this time on the syntax of Javanese. This resulted in a string of articles on the foundations of syntax[18], and in detailed studies of Javanese syntax[19]. Uhlenbeck also recognized the full importance of intonation, which he now wanted to integrate in a theory of syntax, based on the concepts of word grouping and sentence segmentation[20]. For Uhlenbeck sentence segmentation is the articulation of sentences into syntagmatically functioning segments. Such segments contain at least one word and are separated from each other by a potential pause. Whereas word grouping is generally a matter of obligatory rules, sentence segmentation is typically an optional phenomenon. Segmentation does not affect the semantic content of the sentence, which is the result of the phenomenon of word grouping, but rather modulates this content. To this interaction between segmentation and content one can then apply discourse notions like "topic" and "comment". Uhlenbeck expounded his revised theory in a series of articles on sentence segmentation in Javanese[21]; the concept of sentence segmentation also proved useful for the description of older stages of the language[22].

---

[18] See "Traditionele zinsontleding en syntaxis", *Levende Talen* 193 (1958), 18-30; "De beginselen van het syntactisch onderzoek", in A.J.B.N. Reichling *et al.*, *Taalonderzoek in onze tijd* (The Hague, 1962), 17-37; "Betekenis en syntaxis", *Forum der Letteren* 5 (1964), 67-82; (with A. Reichling) "Fundamentals of Syntax", in H.G. Lunt (ed.), *Proceedings of the 9th International Congress of Linguists, Cambridge, Mass., August 27-31, 1962* (The Hague - London - Paris, 1964), 166-171.

[19] See, e.g., the following studies: "Some Preliminary Remarks on Javanese Syntax", *Lingua* 15 (1965), 53-70; "Nouns from Verb Bases, a Transpositional Category in Standard Javanese", in *Nomen: Leyden Studies in Linguistics and Phonetics* (The Hague, 1969), 178-190; "Position and Syntactic Function of the Particle *ta* in Old Javanese", in R. Jakobson - S. Kawamoto (eds.), *Studies in General and Oriental Linguistics Presented to Shirô Hattori on the occasion of his sixtieth birthday* (Tokyo, 1970), 648-658; "Sentence Segment and Word Group, Basic Concepts of Javanese Syntax", in J.W.M. Verhaar (ed.), *Miscellaneous Studies in Indonesian and Languages in Indonesia* (Djakarta, 1975), vol. I, 6-10; "Two Mechanisms of Javanese Syntax: The Construction with *sing (kang, ingkang)* and with *olehe (ĕnggone, anggenipun)*", in A. Halim - L. Carrington - S.A. Wurm (eds.), *Papers from the Third International Conference on Austronesian Linguistics* (Canberra, 1983), vol. 4: *Thematic Variation*, 9-20; "Sentence Patterns in the Old Javanese of the Parwa Literature", in D.C. Laycock - W. Winter (eds.), *A World of Language: Papers presented to Professor S.A. Wurm on his 65th Birthday* (Canberra, 1987), 695-708.

[20] The latter concept is borrowed from Ch. Bally, *Linguistique générale et linguistique française* (Berne, 1944); see E.M. Uhlenbeck, "Sentence Segment and Word Group, Basic Concepts of Javanese Syntax", *a.c.* [see note 19]; "Two Mechanisms of Javanese Syntax: The Construction with *sing (kang, ingkang)* and with *olehe (ĕnggone, anggenipun)*", *a.c.* [see note 19].

[21] See the publications referred to in note 20.

[22] See the publications referred to in note 29.

Uhlenbeck's descriptive work on Javanese was not severed from his historical-comparative research on Austronesian languages. From the late 1950s on he has carried out important work on the languages of Indonesia and Malaysia, on the comparative study of Austronesian, and on the historical relationships within the group[23].

An accomplished descriptive and theoretical linguist Uhlenbeck is also a talented organizer. In 1967, after his stay at the University of California at San Diego and at the Center for Advanced Study in the Behavioral Sciences in Stanford, Uhlenbeck became a member of ZWO, the Dutch national organization for scientific research. Also in 1967 he became a member of the "Raad van Advies voor het Wetenschaps-beleid", of which he was vice-president in 1971[24]. In 1970 he was elected president of the board of the Netherlands Institute for Advanced Study in the Humanities and Social Sciences (NIAS) in Wassenaar[25]. Upon his retirement in 1983 the board expressed its gratitude for his unfailing dedication by initiating a series of annual "Uhlenbeck-lectures", the first of which was given by the scholar to whom the series was dedicated[26]. In 1977 Uhlenbeck joined the Comité International Permanent des Linguistes (CIPL), after having held the office of president of the Societas Linguistica Europaea in 1972. As secretary-general of CIPL he was instrumental in putting the finances on a healthy basis. He was also the driving force behind the international congresses of linguists held in Tokyo (1982), Berlin (1987) and Québec (1992). For the 1992 congress Uhlenbeck put the "Endangered Languages Project" on

---

[23] E.M. Uhlenbeck - A.A. Cense, *Critical Survey of Studies on the Languages of Borneo* (The Hague, 1958); "The Comparative Study of the Austronesian Languages", in H.L. Shorto (ed.), *Linguistic Comparison in South East Asia and the Pacific* (London, 1963), 24-27; *A Critical Survey of Studies on the Languages of Java and Madura* (The Hague, 1964); "Indonesia and Malaysia", in Th. A. Sebeok (ed.), *Current Trends in Linguistics* vol. 2: *Linguistics in East Asia and South East Asia* (The Hague, 1967), 847-898; "Indonesia and Malaysia", in Th. A. Sebeok (ed.), *Current Trends in Linguistics* 8: *Linguistics in Oceania* (The Hague, 1971), 55-111; "The Languages of Indonesia: Past, Present and Future", *Southeast Asia* 1 (1971), 209-221; *Studies in Javanese Morphology* (The Hague, 1978); *Javanese Linguistics, A Retrospect and Some Prospects* (Dordrecht, 1983).

[24] See, e.g., his writings on science policy in the humanities: (& H.C.J. Duijker) *Taalkunde en Sociale Wetenschappen* (Amsterdam, 1975); "Wetenschapsbeleid en geestes-wetenschappelijk onderzoek", in W. de Vroomen (ed.), *Geesteswetenschappelijk onderzoekbeleid* (= *Forum der Letteren* 16/3, 1975), 15-27; "Science Policy and Research in the Humanities", *Research Policy in the Humanities of the Netherlands* (The Hague, 1976), 23-32.

[25] See E.M. Uhlenbeck, "The Birth of NIAS", *22 1/2 Years of NIAS* (Wassenaar, 1994), 15-24.

[26] E.M. Uhlenbeck, *Linguistics: Neither Psychology nor Sociology* (Wassenaar, 1983).

the agenda of CIPL, and this project was subsequently adopted by UNESCO[27].

Within CIPL Uhlenbeck's most significant contribution has been the reorganization of the *Bibliographie Linguistique/Linguistic Bibliography* (*BL*). Uhlenbeck first secured a permanent appointment as senior officer for Johannes J. Beylsmit (1921-1986), and then was instrumental in adding an associate editor to the editorial board of *BL*. In 1985 he saw the achievement of what had been one of his initial goals, viz. reducing the time lag between the year covered and the year of publication to two years. The standard attained by *BL* in the past few years owes very much to Uhlenbeck's initiatives and dedication.

In 1979 Uhlenbeck retired as Professor of General Linguistics at Leiden University, and in 1983 he retired as Professor of Javanese Language and Literature. He has, however, continued to publish actively, both in the field of general linguistics (with special focus on word-based morphology, and on the relationship between syntax and semantics)[28], and in the area of Javanese studies[29].

---

[27] See E.M. Uhlenbeck, "De dreiging van snelle taalsterfte, een sinds kort onderkend mondiaal probleem", *Ons Erfdeel* 36 (1993), 23-31 (English translation: "The Threat of Rapid Language Death, a Recently Acknowledged Global Problem", in *The Low Countries. Arts and society in Flanders and the Netherlands. A Yearbook, 1993-1994* [Brugge, 1993], 25-31); E.M. Uhlenbeck - R.H. Robins (eds.), *Endangered Languages* (Oxford, 1991).

[28] See, e.g., his recent articles: "Why Do All Languages Have a Syntax? The instrumental relationship between syntax and semantics", in S. Rot (ed.), *Languages in Function. Materials of the XIIIth Annual Conference of the Societas Linguistica Europaea, held in Budapest 3-6.IX.1980* (Budapest, 1983), 291-299; "Functioneel-structurele morfologie versus generatieve morfologie", *Forum der Letteren* 28 (1987), 115-122; "Words", in W. Bright (ed.), *International Encyclopedia of Linguistics* (New York - Oxford, 1992), vol. IV, 246-248; "General Linguistics and the Study of Morphological Processes", *Oceanic Linguistics* 31 (1992), 1-11; "Distinctions in the Study of Linguistic Semantics", in A. Heen Wold (ed.), *The Dialogical Alternative. Towards a Theory of Language and Mind* (Oslo, 1992), 273-291; "Some Remarks on Homonymy and Polysemy", in B. H. Partee - P. Sgall (eds.), *Discourse and Meaning. Papers in Honor of Eva Hajičová* (Amsterdam - Philadelphia, 1996), 119-126; "The Concepts of Process, Category, and Productivity in Morphology", in V. Law - W. Hüllen (eds.), *Linguists and Their Diversions* (Münster, 1996), 395-405; "Basic Concepts of Morphological Theory" (forthcoming).

[29] See, e.g., his publications: "Clitic, Suffix, and Particle: Some Indispensable Distinctions in Old Javanese Grammar", in C.M.S. Hellwig - S.O. Robson (eds.), *A Man of Indonesian Letters. Essays in Honour of Professor A. Teeuw* (Dordrecht, 1986), 334-341; "Sentence Patterns in the Old Javanese of the Parwa Literature", in D.C. Laycock - W. Winter (eds.), *A World of Language: Papers presented to Professor S.A. Wurm on his 65th Birthday* (Canberra, 1987), 695-708; "Nouns, Nominal Groups, and Substitutional Processes in Old Javanese", in R. Harlow (ed.), *VICAL vol. 2, Western Austronesian and Contact Languages. Papers from the Fifth International Conference on Austronesian Linguistics* (Auckland, 1991), 349-366; "Antonymic Processes within the System of

In the past two decades Uhlenbeck received several distinctions. In 1972 he was made honorary member of the Linguistic Society of America, and in 1975 he received a doctorate *honoris causa* from the University of Leuven, which was followed in 1991 by another honorary degree from Charles University in Prague. In addition Uhlenbeck was elected as an honorary member of the Royal Institute of Linguistics and Anthropology in Leiden in 1983, as an honorary member of the Cercle Linguistique de Prague in 1991, as the honorary president of the Association of Alumni and Friends of Charles University in 1993, and as an honorary member of the British Academy in 1994.

Uhlenbeck's theory of general linguistics can be defined as a compre-hensive and realistic linguistics, which takes into account both *language use* and *language analysis* (and theorization), and as a sign- or word-based theory. For Uhlenbeck words are the central units in the language system and in the use made of the system by the speakers: we speak by using words, the units through which sentences are constructed[30]. The construction of sentences is always an activity which involves meaning: semantics and syntax are interrelated[31]. This is apparent from the phenom-enon of word grouping (i.e. syntax in its strictest sense): word grouping installs a semantic interaction between the words combined, thus limit-ing their inherent flexibility, and it permits speakers to create a theoreti-cally unlimited number of *ad hoc* units on the basis of a relatively small vocabulary, thus increasing the referential capacity of language without putting too heavy a burden on the speaker's memory.

The centrality of the word appears from its contribution to syntax and from its structuring role in morphology. Here the notion of proportional-ity, which Uhlenbeck borrowed from Prague School phonology, has been crucially important[32]. Proportionality is a relationship between (series

Javanese Adjectives", in T. Dutton - M. Ross - D. Tryon (eds.), *The Language Game: Papers in Memory of Donald C. Laycock* (Canberra, 1992), 491-500; "Functional Sentence Perspective in Modern and Old Javanese", in S. Čmejrková - F. Štícha (eds.), *The Syntax of Sentence and Text. A Festschrift for František Daneš* (Amsterdam - Philadelphia, 1994), 179-192; "Old Javanese Word Structure" (forthcoming).

[30] See E.M. Uhlenbeck, "De positie van woord en zin in taal en taalwetenschap", *Neerlandica extra muros* 32:2 (1994), 1-9.

[31] See E.M. Uhlenbeck, "Betekenis in linguïstisch perspectief", *Mededelingen der KNAW, Afd. Letterkunde*, N.S. 44 (1981), 339-360 [also published separately]; "Why Do All Languages Have a Syntax? The instrumental relationship between syntax and semantics", *a.c.* [see note 28].

[32] E.M. Uhlenbeck, "The Concept of Proportionality, Old Javanese Morphology and the Structure of the Old Javanese Word *kakawin*", in S. Sutrisno - Darusuprapta - Sudaryanto (eds.), *Bahasa - Sastra - Budaya, ratna manikam untaian persembahan kepada Prof. Dr. P.J. Zoetmulder* (Yogyakarta, 1985), 66-82; "Basic Concepts of Morphological Theory" (forthcoming).

of) words determining and defining category membership. On the basis of the proportions *big: bigger*, *great: greater*, *large: larger*, the simple words *big*, *great* and *large* are included in the adjective system. At the same time, these proportions are used to establish one of the three categories of comparison, viz. the comparative. It is important to realize that in Uhlenbeck's opinion proportionality is a relationship between words, not between morphemes. Given his view of language as a system used to convey meaning, Uhlenbeck uses proportional relationships only when these involve simultaneously word form and word meaning. Hence there is no proportionality between the two series *big: bigger* and *sing: singer*.

For Uhlenbeck the basic subject matter of linguistics is the analysis of the act of speech, set in its communicative context[33]. This involves, on the one hand, the rejection of the distinction between competence and performance, and on the other hand, the recognition that language always functions in conjunction with extralinguistic knowledge such as knowledge about the situation in which speaking takes place, knowledge about its participants and, generally, knowledge about the (real and/or imaginary) world which speaker and hearer share. Linguistics, the study of lingual signs, deals with "open" systems[34], in which meaning is intrinsically linked to form. Uhlenbeck has made it clear that his approach of language radically departs from all code-based conceptions of language: "Characterization of a language as a code, is misleading both because of its structure and because of the way it is used. Every language is structured in such a way that it gives every native speaker the means for productive and creative use within a framework of obligatory syntactic, morphological and phonological rules. The syntactic rules allow combinatorial semantic freedom, the morphological rules describe productive procédés available to every speaker, and word meaning is a form of knowledge that can be creatively used in various ways (e.g. metaphor). Every language is a functional structure of which obligatoriness and freedom are design features. Language is always used

---

[33] See E.M. Uhlenbeck, "Language in Action", in *To Honor Roman Jakobson. Essays on the occasion of his seventieth birthday, 11 October 1966* (The Hague, 1967), 2060-2066; "The Dynamic Nature of Word Meaning", *Actes du Xᵉ Congrès international des linguistes, Bucarest, 28 août - 2 septembre 1967* (Bucarest, 1970), II, 679-684; "The Communicative Function of Language and Speech", in F. Coppieters - D.L. Goyvaerts (eds.), *Functional Studies in Language and Literature* (Antwerp, 1978), 109-117; "The Linguistic Senselessness of the Concept of Nonsense-Sentences", *International Journal of American Linguistics* 51: 4 (1985), 602-604.

[34] See E.M. Uhlenbeck, "Observation in Semantics is Not Easy", in D.J. van Alkemade - A. Feitsma - W.J. Meys - P. van Reenen - J.J. Spa (eds.), *Linguistic Studies Offered to Berthe Siertsema* (Amsterdam, 1980), 127-135; "Some Remarks on Homonymy and Polysemy", *a.c.* [see note 28].

in conjunction with extra-lingual information from different sources. The speaker assumes that the hearer will be able to infer from the linguistic information inherent in what the speaker says, and from the extralingual sources at the hearer's disposal, what the speaker wants to convey him. Conversely, the hearer always assumes that the speaker wants to convey something to him, and that the speaker apparently believes that he, the hearer, is able to determine what this is"[35].

---

[35] E.M. Uhlenbeck, "First Principles in the Study of Language", in D. Seleskovitch (ed.), *Comprendre le langage* (Paris, 1981), 86-88.

E.M. UHLENBECK: BIBLIOGRAPHICAL NOTICE

1941

1. *Beknopte Javaansche grammatica*. Batavia: Volkslectuur. 107 pp.
2. "Interessante vertalingen". *Tijdschrift van het Koninklijk Bataviaasch Genootschap van Kunsten en Wetenschappen* 81. 295-306.
3. "De plaats van de Moedertaal, het Nederlandsch en het Maleisch". *Indisch Weekblad*, 26 september 1941, p. 10.

1948

4. "De betekenis van de phonologie". *Tijdschrift van het Koninklijk Bataviaasch Genootschap van Kunsten en Wetenschappen* 82. 312-329.

1949

5. *De structuur van het Javaanse morpheem* (Verhandelingen van het Koninklijk Bataviaasch Genootschap van Kunsten en Wetenschappen 78). Bandoeng: Nix. 240 pp. [= Ph.D. Leiden]

1950

6. *De tegenstelling Krama: Ngoko. Haar positie in het Javaanse taalsysteem*. Groningen/Jakarta: Wolters. 28 p.
7. "The Structure of the Javanese Morpheme". *Lingua* 2. 239-270. [Reprinted: E.P. Hamp - F.W. Householder - R. Austerlitz (eds.), *Readings in Linguistics II*, Chicago: University of Chicago Press, 1966, 248-270.]
8. R: C.F.P. Stutterheim, *Inleiding tot de Taalphilosophie. Tijdschrift voor Nederlandse Taal- en Letterkunde* 68. 234-240.

1951

9. R: J.H.M.C. Boelaers, *The Linguistic Position of South-Western New Guinea. Bijdragen tot de Taal-, Land- en Volkenkunde* 107. 90-92.
10. R: *Bingkisan Budi* (Festschrift Ph.S. van Ronkel). *Bijdragen tot de Taal-, Land- en Volkenkunde* 107. 92-94.
11. R: *Bibliographie linguistique 1939-1947. Bijdragen tot de Taal-, Land- en Volkenkunde* 107. 94.

1952

12. R: D.W.N. de Boer, *Beknopte Indonesische grammatica, van klassiek naar modern Maleis. Bijdragen tot de Taal-, Land- en Volkenkunde* 108. 205-206.

13. R: P.J. Zoetmulder, *De taal van het Adiparwa. Bijdragen tot de Taal-, Land- en Volkenkunde* 108. 305-311.
14. R: A.W. de Groot, *Structurele Syntaxis. Museum* 57. 66-68.

1953

15. "The Study of Word Classes in Javanese". *Lingua* 3. 322-354.
16. "Woordverdubbeling in het Javaans". *Bijdragen tot de Taal-, Land- en Volkenkunde* 109. 52-61.
17. "De systematiek der Javaanse telwoorden". *Bijdragen tot de Taal-, Land- en Volkenkunde* 109. 342-375.
18. "Het aandeel van phonetiek en phonologie in het onderzoek van onbekende talen". *Nederlandse Vereniging voor Phonetische Wetenschappen; verslagen van vergaderingen in 1953*. 12-15.

1954

19. "Verdubbelingsprocédé's bij het Javaanse werkwoord". *Bijdragen tot de Taal-, Land- en Volkenkunde* 110. 369-387.
20. (& H. Mol) "The Analysis of the Phoneme in Distinctive Features and the Process of Hearing". *Lingua* 4. 167-193.
21. R: *Bibliographie linguistique 1951. Museum* 59. 145.

1955

22. "Over woordvorming in het Javaans". *Bijdragen tot de Taal-, Land- en Volkenkunde* 111. 286-307.
23. (& H. Mol) "The Linguistic Relevance of Intensity in Stress". *Lingua* 5. 205-213.
24. R: W. Porzig, *Das Wunder der Sprache. Museum* 60. 17-19.
25. R: I. Dyen, *Proto-Malayo-Polynesian Laryngeals. Lingua* 5. 308-318. [1956]

1956

26. "Verb Structure in Javanese". M. Halle - H.G. Lunt - H. McLean - C.H. van Schooneveld (eds.), *For Roman Jakobson. Essays on the occasion of his sixtieth birthday, 11 October 1956*, 567-573. The Hague: Mouton.
27. "De studie der zgn. exotische talen in verband met de algemene taalwetenschap". *Museum* 61. 65-80.
28. "Taalwetenschap". E.J. Dijksterhuis ed., *Scientia. Handboek voor wetenschap, kunst en religie*, I, 258-275. Zeist: De Haan.
29. "Het onderzoek der intonatie-verschijnselen". *Handelingen van het vierentwintigste Nederlands Filologencongres (Amsterdam, 5-6 april 1956)*, 77-78.
30. R: P. Guiraud, *Bibliographie critique de la statistique linguistique. Lingua* 6. 203-209.

31. R: *Bibliographie linguistique 1952; Bibliographie linguistique 1953. Museum* 61. 81-82.

1957

32. (& A.W. de Groot) "Some Impressions of the 8th International Congress of Linguists Held in Oslo, Norway, August 5-9 1957". *Lingua* 7. 87-98.
33. (& H. Mol) "The Correlation between Interpretation and Production of Speech Sounds". *Lingua* 6. 333-353.
34. R: J.B. Carroll, *The Study of Language. A survey of linguistics and related disciplines in America. Romance Philology* 10. 343-347.

1958

35. (& A.A. Cense) ***Critical Survey of Studies on the Languages of Borneo*** (Bibliographical Series of the Royal Institute of Linguistics and Anthropology 2). The Hague: Nijhoff. 82 pp.
36. "Traditionele zinsontleding en syntaxis". *Levende Talen* 193. 18-30.
37. (& A. Teeuw) "Over de interpretatie van de Nāgarakṛtāgama". *Bijdragen tot de Taal-, Land- en Volkenkunde* 114. 210-237.
38. (& S. Dresden) "De noodzaak van het vertalen". *Museum* 63. 225-236. [Reprinted in: T. Naaykens (ed.), *Vertalers als erflaters; staalkaart van een eeuw vertalen*, 181-194. Bussem: Coutinho, 1996.]
39. "De universitaire studie in de zgn. moderne talen". *Universiteit en Hogeschool* 4. 258-265.

1959

40. ***Taalwetenschap, een eerste inleiding***. The Hague: Smits. 47 pp. [1980⁹, 116 pp.] [Indonesian translation: 1982, *Ilmu bahasa, pengantar dasar*. Jakarta: Djambatan. ix-90 pp.]
41. "Syntaxis te Sappemeer". *De Nieuwe Taalgids* 52. 222-223.
42. (& H. Mol) "Hearing and the Concept of the Phoneme". *Lingua* 8. 161-185.
43. "Die mit javanisch *rasa* morphologisch zusammenhängenden Wörter. Ein Beitrag zur javanischen Lexikologie". *Oriens Extremus* 6. 104-115.
44. R: M. Joos (ed.), *Readings in Linguistics. The development of descriptive linguistics in America since 1925. Lingua* 8. 327-329.

1960

45. ***Aantekeningen bij Tjan Tjoe Siem's vertaling van de Lakon Kurupati Rabi*** (Verhandelingen van het Koninklijk Instituut voor Taal-, Land- en Volkenkunde 29). The Hague: Nijhoff. viii + 67 pp.

46. *De systematiek der Javaanse pronomina* (Verhandelingen van het Koninklijk Instituut voor Taal-, Land- en Volkenkunde 30). The Hague: Nijhoff. viii + 63 pp.
47. "The Study of the So-Called Exotic Languages and General Linguistics". *Lingua* 9. 417-434. [English version of 27]
48. "Moderne Nederlandse taalbeschrijving. Een critiek". *Forum der Letteren* 1. 56-69.
49. R: M.E.J.G. Verstraelen, *De bijwoordelijke bepalingen van het werkwoord in enkele Indonesische talen. Bijdragen tot de Taal-, Land- en Volkenkunde* 116. 388-390.
50. R: A. Capell, *A Linguistic Survey of the South-Western Pacific. Bijdragen tot de Taal-, Land- en Volkenkunde* 116. 391-392.
51. R: C. Maxwell Churchward, *Tongan Grammar + Tongan Dictionary. Bijdragen tot de Taal-, Land- en Volkenkunde* 116. 392.
52. R: H.R. Klieneberger, *Bibliography of Oceanic Linguistics. Bijdragen tot de Taal-, Land- en Volkenkunde* 116. 393.

1961

53. "Het 10de Pacific Science Congress van 21 augustus tot 6 september te Honolulu gehouden". *Bijdragen tot de Taal-, Land- en Volkenkunde* 117. 475-478.

1962

54. "Enige kanttekeningen bij Lochers artikel over Lévi-Strauss". *Forum der Letteren* 3. 48-53.
55. "Limitations of Morphological Processes. Some preliminary remarks". *Lingua* 11 [= Festschrift A.W. de Groot]. 426-432.
56. "De beginselen van het syntactisch onderzoek". A.J.B.N. Reichling *et al.*, *Taalonderzoek in onze tijd*, 17-37. The Hague: Servire. [Reprinted in: J. Hoogteijling (ed.), *Taalkunde in artikelen*, 24-43. Groningen: Wolters - Noordhoff, 1968.]

1963

57. "An Appraisal of Transformation Theory". *Lingua* 12. 1-18.
58. "The Comparative Study of the Austronesian Languages". H.L. Shorto (ed.), *Linguistic Comparison in South East Asia and the Pacific*, 24-27. London: School of Oriental and African Studies.
58a. (Editors *Lingua*:) "Albert Willem de Groot 13 Jan. 1892 - 14 Dec. 1963". *Lingua* 12. 229-232.
59. R: E.C. Horne, *Beginning Javanese. Lingua* 12. 69-86.
60. R: A.J.J. de Witte - N.C.H. Wijngaards, *De struktuur van het Nederlands. Levende Talen* 220. 411-420.

1964

61. **A Critical Survey of Studies on the Languages of Java and Madura.**
    (Bibliographical Series of the Royal Institute of Linguistics and
    Anthropology 7). The Hague: Nijhoff. viii + 207 pp.
62. "Betekenis en syntaxis". *Forum der Letteren* 5. 67-82. [Reprinted
    in: J. Hoogteijling (ed.), *Taalkunde in artikelen*, 44-59. Groningen:
    Wolters - Noordhoff, 1968.]
63. (& A. Reichling) "Fundamentals of Syntax". H.G. Lunt (ed.), *Pro-
    ceedings of the 9th International Congress of Linguists, Cambridge,
    Mass., August 27-31, 1962*, 166-171. The Hague/London/Paris:
    Mouton.
64. "Commentaar" (op C. Kruyskamp in de NRC over spelling). *Forum
    der Letteren* 5. 91-94.

1965

65. "Some Preliminary Remarks on Javanese Syntax". *Lingua* 15 [=
    Indo-Pacific Linguistic Studies II: Descriptive Linguistics]. 53-
    70.
66. (& J.C. Anceaux) "On Melanesian and the Origin of Austronesian.
    (Some comments on Capell's 'Oceanic linguistics to-day')".
    Current Anthropology 6. 222-223.
67. R: C. Mohrmann - A. Sommerfelt - J. Whatmough (eds.), *Trends in
    European and American Linguistics 1930-1960*; C. Mohrmann - F. Nor-
    man - A. Sommerfelt (eds.), *Trends in Modern Linguistics. Romance
    Philology* 19. 353-360.

1966

68. "Enige beschouwingen over Amerikaanse en Nederlandse linguïs-
    tiek". *Forum der Letteren* 7. 1-22.
69. "Substantief + substantief in Modern Algemeen Nederlands, een
    begin van syntactische beschrijving". *De Nieuwe Taalgids* 59. 291-
    301. [Post-scriptum: *De Nieuwe Taalgids* 63. 1970. 114-115]
    [Reprinted in: J. Hoogteijling (ed.), *Taalkunde in artikelen*, 175-
    185. Groningen: Wolters - Noordhoff, 1968.]

1967

70. "Indonesia and Malaysia". Th. A. Sebeok (ed.), *Current Trends in
    Linguistics* vol. 2: *Linguistics in East Asia and South East Asia*,
    847-898. The Hague: Mouton.
71. "Some Further Remarks on Transformational Grammar". *Lingua*
    17. 263-316. [Russian translation: "Ešče raz o transformacionnoj
    grammatike". *Voprosy Jazykoznanija* 1968/3. 94-111; 1968/4. 107-116]

72. "Language in Action". *To Honor Roman Jakobson. Essays on the occasion of his seventieth birthday, 11 October 1966*, 2060-2066. The Hague: Mouton.
73. "Perspectief der Nederlandse Oriëntalistiek". *Bijdragen tot de Taal-, Land- en Volkenkunde* 123. 205-216. [Japanese translation in: *Kokugakuin Zasshi. The Journal of Kokugakuin University* 70/12 (1969). 34-53.]
74. "In Dresdens Wereld in Woorden". *Forum der Letteren* 8. 55-62.
75. (Review article on:) *L'école de Prague d'aujourd'hui. Travaux linguistiques de Prague* 1. *Lingua* 17. 358-365.
76. (Review article on:) G. Mounin, *Les problèmes théoriques de la traduction. Lingua* 18. 196-206.
76a. R: Th. G. Pigeaud, *Literature of Java. Forum der Letteren* 8. 231-233.
77. R: *Betekenis en Betekenisstructuur. Nagelaten geschriften van Prof. Dr. A.W. de Groot* (ed. G.F. Bos - H. Roose). *Forum der Letteren* 8. 233-240.

1968

78. (& S.C. Dik & J.G. Kooij) "Some Impressions of the 10th International Congress of Linguists". *Lingua* 19. 225-232.
79. "Personal Pronouns and Pronominal Suffixes in Old Javanese". *Lingua* 21 [= Festschrift in Honour of A.J.B.N. Reichling]. 466-482.
80. "Taalonderwijs en taalonderzoek". *Forum der Letteren* 9. 65-80.

1969

81. "Nouns from Verb Bases, a Transpositional Category in Standard Javanese". *Nomen, Leyden Studies in Linguistics and Phonetics*, 178-190. The Hague/Paris: Mouton.
82. "On the Notion of 'Completely Novel Sentences'". *Cahiers Ferdinand de Saussure* 26 [= Festschrift Henri Frei II]. 179-186. [1971]
83. "Systematic Features of Javanese Personal Names". *Word* 25 [= *Linguistic Studies Presented to André Martinet*]. 321-335.
84. [Commentaar:] "Studie van taalfunctiestoornissen te Leiden zonder taalfunctie-deskundigen". *Forum der Letteren* 10. 55-56.
85. R: A. van Gennep, *The Semi-Scholars. Bijdragen tot de Taal-, Land- en Volkenkunde* 125. 157.
86. R: A. Teeuw, *Modern Indonesian Literature. Forum der Letteren* 10. 58-59.

1970

87. "The Dynamic Nature of Word Meaning". *Actes du Xᵉ Congrès international des linguistes, Bucarest, 28 août - 2 septembre 1967*, II, 679-684. Bucarest: Académie de la République socialiste de Roumanie.

88. "Facts and Theory in the Study of So-Called Adverbs and Adverbials in Present-Day English". J. Dierickx - Y. Lebrun (eds.), *Linguistique contemporaine. Hommage à Eric Buyssens*, 253-260. Bruxelles: Institut de Sociologie.

89. "Position and Syntactic Function of the Particle *ta* in Old Javanese". R. Jakobson - S. Kawamoto (eds.), *Studies in General and Oriental Linguistics Presented to Shirô Hattori on the occasion of his sixtieth birthday*, 648-658. Tokyo: TEC.

90. "The Use of Respect Forms in Javanese". S.A. Wurm - D.C. Laycock (eds.), *Pacific Linguistic Studies in Honour of Arthur Capell*, 441-466. Canberra: Australian National University. (Pacific Linguistics, series C-13)

91. "Taalwetenschap en taalonderwijs". *Forum der Letteren* 11. 94-99.

92. The Need for Transparency in Language Description. Paper for the Burg Wartenstein Symposium no 49: *Toward the Description of the Languages of the World*, August 1-8, 1970. 21 pp. New York: Wenner-Gren Foundation for Anthropological Research.

93. "The Javanese Verb System". *Proceedings of the 26th International Congress of Orientalists, New Delhi, 4-10 January 1964*, vol. IV, 79-84.

94. R: *To Honor Roman Jakobson. Essays on the occasion of his seventieth birthday. Forum der Letteren* 11. 71-75.

1971

95. "Nové výsledky vývoje transformační generativní gramatiky (kritický přehled; hodnocení)" [With summary: 'Recent Developments in Transformational Generative Grammar']. *Slovo a Slovesnost* 32. 1-19, 117-139.

96. "Peripheral Verb Categories with Emotive-Expressive or Onomatopoeic Value in Modern Javanese". *Travaux linguistiques de Prague* 4 [= Festschrift J. Vachek & V. Skalička]. 145-156.

97. "Kraak's negatieve zinnen. Een laat antwoord". *Forum der Letteren* 12. 100-134.

98. "Indonesia and Malaysia". Th. A. Sebeok (ed.), *Current Trends in Linguistics* vol. 8: *Linguistics in Oceania*, 55-111. The Hague: Mouton.

99. "The Languages of Indonesia: Past, Present and Future". *Southeast Asia* 1. 209-221.

1972

100. R: P.E. de Josselin de Jong, *Contact der continenten. Bijdrage tot het begrijpen van niet-westerse samenlevingen. Bijdragen tot de Taal-, Land- en Volkenkunde* 128. 148-151.

1973

101. ***Critical Comments on Transformational-Generative Grammar 1962-1972***. The Hague: Smits. viii-171 pp. [Contains nos. 57, 71, 82, 95 + "Semantic Representation and Word Meaning"]
102. (& T.J.M. van Els) "Het universitair onderwijs in de moderne vreemde talen. Rapport van de commissie ad hoc inzake de vernieuwing van het onderwijs in de moderne vreemde talen". *Levende Talen* 300. 429-445.

1974

103. "Structurele Taalwetenschap". F. Balk-Smit Duyzentkunst *et al.*, *Controversen in de taal- en literatuurwetenschap*, 137-168. Wassenaar: Servire.

1975

104. (& H.C.J. Duijker) ***Taalkunde en Sociale Wetenschappen***. (Koninklijke Nederlandse Akademie van Wetenschappen: Sociaal-Wetenschappelijke Raad, Werkdocumenten, 4). Amsterdam: Noord-Hollandsche Uitgeversmaatschappij. 44 pp.
105. "De interpretatie van de Oud-Javaanse Rāmāyaṇa-kakawin. Enige algemene beschouwingen en gezichtspunten". *Bijdragen tot de Taal-, Land- en Volkenkunde* 131. 195-213.
106. "Sentence Segment and Word Group, Basic Concepts of Javanese Syntax". J.W.M. Verhaar (ed.), *Miscellaneous Studies in Indonesian and Languages in Indonesia* vol. I, 6-10. Jakarta: Badan Penyelenggara Seri NUSA.
107. "Transformational-Generative Grammar and the Teaching of Foreign Languages: A Critical Appraisal". A.J. van Essen - J.P. Menting (eds.), *The Context of Foreign-Language Learning*, 152-158. Assen: van Gorcum.
108. "Wetenschapsbeleid en geesteswetenschappelijk onderzoek". W. de Vroomen (ed.), *Geesteswetenschappelijk onderzoekbeleid* (= *Forum der Letteren* 16/3). 15-27.
109. "Aspecten van het wetenschapsbeleid". *Koninklijke Nederlandse Akademie van Wetenschappen, Verslag Bijzondere zitting van de beide afdelingen op 24 mei 1975*. 9-18.
110. "Meer aandacht voor de Nederlandse graduate school". *Niet bij wetenschap alleen … Liber amicorum aangeboden aan dr. A.J. Piekaar, bij zijn afscheid als directeur-generaal van het Ministerie van Onderwijs en Wetenschappen op 27 februari 1975*, 134-140. Den Haag: Ministerie van Onderwijs en Wetenschappen.
111. [Commentaar:] "Een zwarte dag voor de didactiek in Leiden". *Forum der Letteren* 16. 66-69.

112. [Commentaar:] "De Romaanse talen in Illinois". "Niet ter diskussie in de taalwetenschap?" "Onderzoek van onderzoek van onderwijs gewenst". "Professor Freudenthal's kleinzoontje verdedigd tegen zijn grootvader". *Forum der Letteren* 16. 249-254.
113. "Wanbegrip over aard en functie van de Oriëntalistiek". *NRC Handelsblad*, June 7 1975.

1976

114. *Taal en Taalwetenschap*. Leiden: Universitaire Pers. 20 pp.
115. "Javanese Kinship and Forms of Respect". *Archív Orientální* 44. 253-266.
116. "Science Policy and Research in the Humanities". *Research Policy in the Humanities of the Netherlands*, 23-32. The Hague: Staatsuitgeverij.
117. "Wetenschapsbeleid en geesteswetenschappelijk onderzoek". W. Hutter *et al.* (eds.), *Op weg naar criteria voor onderzoeksbeleid* (= *OTO Cahiers* 1), 136-141. Groningen: Wolters-Noordhoff.

1977

118. "Roman Jakobson and Dutch Linguistics". D. Armstrong - C.H. van Schooneveld (eds.), *Roman Jakobson: Echoes of his Scholarship*, 485-502. Lisse: Peter de Ridder.
119. "The Concepts of Productivity and Potentiality in Morphological Description and their Psycholinguistic Reality". G. Drachman (ed.), *Akten der 3. Salzburger Jahrestagung für Linguistik (Psycholinguistik) 1976*, 379-392. Salzburg: Neugebauer.
120. "Nederlandse voorlichting over generatieve grammatica". *Forum der Letteren* 18. 167-210.

1978

121. *Studies in Javanese Morphology*. (Translation Series of the Royal Institute of Linguistics and Anthropology 19). The Hague: Nijhoff. vi + 361 p. [Indonesian translation, 1982, *Kajian morfologi bahasa Jawa*. Jakarta: Djambatan. xiv-417 pp.]
122. "On the Distinction between Linguistics and Pragmatics". D. Gerver - H.W. Sinaiko (eds.), *Language Interpretation and Communication*, 185-198. New York/London: Plenum.
123. "A Classical Case of Structural Ambiguity or No Ambiguity at All?". M.A. Jazayery - E.C. Polomé - W. Winter (eds.), *Linguistic and Literary Studies in Honor of Archibald A. Hill*, vol. II: *Descriptive Linguistics*, 121-125. The Hague: Mouton.

124. "The Communicative Function of Language and Speech". F. Coppieters - D.L. Goyvaerts (eds.), *Functional Studies in Language and Literature*, 109-117. Antwerp: University of Antwerp.

1979

125. "Linguistics in America 1924-1974. A Detached View". H.M. Hoenigswald (ed.), *The European Background of American Linguistics. Papers of the Third Golden Anniversary Symposium of the Linguistic Society of America, December 27, 1974*, 121-144, 153-157. Dordrecht: Foris.
126. "Hoe een linguïst omgaat met ambassadrices en masseuses. Een kritische vergelijking van morfologische theorie en descriptieve praktijk". T. Hoekstra - H. van der Hulst (eds.), *Morfologie in Nederland* (special issue of *Glot*), 7-20.
127. "Schriftelijk en mondeling taalgebruik. Een poging tot analyse van hun fundamentele verschillen". *Forum der Letteren* 20 [= E. van der Starre - F.F.J. Drijkoningen - W. Zwanenburg (eds.), *Lezen en interpreteren, een bundel opstellen voor S. Dresden*]. 405-411.

1980

128. ***Het wonder van de natuurlijke taal.*** (Haarlemse Voordrachten 40). Haarlem: Hollandsche Maatschappij der Wetenschappen. 27 p.
129. "Language Universals, Individual Language Structure, and the *Lingua* Descriptive Series Project". G. Brettschneider - Ch. Lehmann (eds.), *Wege zur Universalienforschung. Sprachwissenschaftliche Beiträge zum 60. Geburtstag von Hansjakob Seiler*, 59-64. Tübingen: Narr.
130. "Observation in Semantics is Not Easy". D.J. van Alkemade - A. Feitsma - W.J. Meys - P. van Reenen - J.J. Spa (eds.), *Linguistic Studies Offered to Berthe Siertsema*, 127-135. Amsterdam: Rodopi.

1981

131. ***Betekenis in linguïstisch perspectief.*** (Mededelingen der Koninklijke Nederlandse Akademie van Wetenschappen, Afd. Letterkunde, Nieuwe reeks 44, no. 8). Amsterdam: Noord-Hollandsche Uitgeversmaatschappij. 24 p. [= "Betekenis in linguïstisch perspectief". *Mededelingen der Koninklijke Nederlandse Akademie van Wetenschappen, Afd. Letterkunde, Nieuwe reeks* 44, 339-360].
132. "First Principles in the Study of Language". D. Seleskovitch (ed.), *Comprendre le langage*, 86-88. Paris.
133. "Language and Linguistics in (Dutch) Structural Anthropology". G.A. Moyer - D.S. Moyer - P.E. de Josselin de Jong (eds.), *The Nature of Structure* (ICA Publication 45), 79-94. Leiden: Institute of Cultural and Social Studies.

134. "Productivity and Creativity, Some Remarks on the Dynamic Aspects of Language". W. Dietrich - H. Geckeler - B. Schlieben-Lange - J. Trabant - H. Weydt (eds.), *Logos Semantikos. Studia Linguistica in Honorem Eugenio Coseriu 1921-1981*, vol. III: *Semantik*, 165-174. Berlin /New York /Madrid: de Gruyter - Gredos.

135. "A Sad Case of Lack of Scholarly Communication: An American Introduction to Old Javanese". *Bijdragen tot de Taal-, Land- en Volkenkunde* 137. 347-362.

1982

136. (& N.G. de Bruijn & W.J.M. Levelt) **Computers in het onderwijs**. [Advice to the Minister of Education and Sciences]. The Hague: Staatsuitgeverij. 20 pp.

137. "Enige beschouwingen over verleden, heden en toekomst van de taalwetenschap in Nederland". *Forum der Letteren* 23. 163-183.

1983

138. **Javanese Linguistics, A Retrospect and Some Prospects**. Lecture delivered on the occasion of the Fourth European Colloquium on Malay and Indonesian Studies on Tuesday May 31 1983. With a foreword by A. Teeuw. Dordrecht: Koninklijk Instituut voor Taal-, Land- en Volkenkunde / Foris. 24 pp.

139. **Linguistics: Neither Psychology nor Sociology**. (Uhlenbeck-Lecture 1). Wassenaar: NIAS. 24 pp.

140. "Two Mechanisms of Javanese Syntax: The Construction with *sing* (*kang*, *ingkang*) and with *olehe* (*ĕnggone*, *anggenipun*)". A. Halim - L. Carrington - S.A. Wurm (eds.), *Papers from the Third International Conference on Austronesian Linguistics*, vol. 4: *Thematic Variation*, 9-20. Canberra: Australian National University. (Pacific Linguistics, series C-77)

141. "Why Do All Languages Have a Syntax? The instrumental relationship between syntax and semantics". S. Rot (ed.), *Languages in Function. Materials of the XIIIth Annual Conference of the Societas Linguistica Europaea, held in Budapest 3-6.IX.1980*, 291-299. Budapest: Sokszorosító.

142. (Review article on:) Tjan Tjoe Siem, *Javaansche kaartspelen. Bijdrage tot de beschrijving van land en volk* (1941). *Bijdragen tot de Taal-, Land- en Volkenkunde* 139. 348-356.

142a. Introduction to: P.J. Zoetmulder, *De taal van het Adiparwa, een grammaticale studie van het Oudjavaans* (1983[2]), v-vi. Dordrecht: Koninklijk Instituut voor Taal-, Land- en Volkenkunde / Foris.

1984

143. "Synthesis and Evaluation". C. Reedijk - C.K. Henry - W.R.H. Koops (eds.), *Large Libraries and New Technological Developments: Proceedings of a Symposium held on the occasion of the inauguration of the new building of the Royal Library, The Hague, 29 September - 1 October 1982*, 179-187. München/New York/London/ Paris: Saur.

144. Preface and Introduction to: F.S. Eringa, *Soendaas-Nederlands Woordenboek*, vii-x, xi-xii. Dordrecht: Koninklijk Instituut voor Taal-, Land- en Volkenkunde / Foris.

1985

145. "The Linguistic Senselessness of the Concept of Nonsense-Sentences". *International Journal of American Linguistics* 51: 4 [= Festschrift Eric P. Hamp]. 602-604.

146. "John opened the door with the key. Some Remarks on Case, Semantic Role and Word Meaning". U. Pieper - G. Stickel (eds.), *Studia Linguistica Diachronica et Synchronica Werner Winter sexagenario anno MCMLXXXIII gratis animis ab eius collegis, amicis discipulisque oblata*, 829-840. Berlin/New York: de Gruyter.

147. "The Concept of Proportionality, Old Javanese Morphology and the Structure of the Old Javanese word *kakawin*". Sulastin Sutrisno - Darusuprapta - Sudaryanto (eds.), *Bahasa - Sastra - Budaya, ratna manikam untaian persembahan kepada Prof. Dr. P.J. Zoetmulder*, 66-82. Yogyakarta: Gadjah Mada University Press.

1986

148. ***De niet-westerse studies in Nederland. Een verkenning***. Zoetermeer: Ministerie van Onderwijs en Wetenschappen. 49 pp.

149. "Clitic, Suffix, and Particle: Some Indispensable Distinctions in Old Javanese Grammar". C.M.S. Hellwig - S.O. Robson (eds.), *A Man of Indonesian Letters. Essays in Honour of Professor A. Teeuw* (= Verhandelingen van het Koninklijk Instituut voor Taal-, Land- en Volkenkunde 121), 334-341. Dordrecht: Foris.

150. "De Jong over Balai Pustaka. Een kritisch commentaar". *Bijdragen tot de Taal-, Land- en Volkenkunde* 142. 337-341.

1987

151. "Sentence Patterns in the Old Javanese of the Parwa Literature". D.C. Laycock - W. Winter (eds.), *A World of Language: Papers presented to Professor S.A. Wurm on his 65th Birthday*, 695-708. Canberra: Australian National University. (Pacific Linguistics, series C-100)

152. "Functioneel-structurele morfologie versus generatieve morfologie". *Forum der Letteren* 28. 115-122.

1988

153. "Anton Reichling: Nijmegen 9 juli 1898 - Amsterdam 25 mei 1986". *Jaarboek van de Maatschappij der Nederlandse Letterkunde te Leiden 1986-1987*. 110-120.

1989

154. "The Problem of Interpolation in the Old Javanese Rāmāyaṇa kakawin". *Bijdragen tot de Taal-, Land- en Volkenkunde* 145. 324-335.
155. "Gebrekkige voorlichting". *Forum der Letteren* 30. 50-53.

1990

156. "Clitics, Morphemes, and Words: Their Structural Differences". W. Bahner - J. Schildt - D. Viehweger (eds.), *Proceedings of the 14th International Congress of Linguists, Berlin/GDR, August 10 - August 15, 1987*, 637-641. Berlin: Akademie-Verlag.

1991

157. "Linguistics, Interpretation, and the Study of Literature". J.J. Ras - S.O. Robson (eds.), *Variation, Transformation and Meaning. Studies on Indonesian Literatures in Honour of A. Teeuw* (= Verhandelingen van het Koninklijk Instituut voor Taal-, Land- en Volkenkunde 144), 17-36. Leiden: Koninklijk Instituut voor Taal-, Land- en Volkenkunde.
158. "Nouns, Nominal Groups, and Substitutional Processes in Old Javanese". R. Harlow (ed.), *VICAL* vol. 2, *Western Austronesian and Contact Languages. Papers from the Fifth International Conference on Austronesian Linguistics*, 349-366. Auckland: Linguistic Society of New Zealand / University of Auckland.
159. "Cornelis Christiaan Berg, 18 december 1900-25 juni 1990". *Jaarboek Koninklijke Nederlandse Akademie van Wetenschappen 1991*, 131-136.
160. (& R.H. Robins) Preface to: R.H. Robins - E.M. Uhlenbeck (eds.), *Endangered Languages*, xiii-xiv. Oxford: Berg.
161. R: S. Daalder - J. Noordegraaf (eds.), *H.J. Pos (1898-1955), taalkundige en geëngageerd filosoof. Ons Erfdeel* 34. 464-465.

1992

162. "Words". W. Bright (ed.), *International Encyclopedia of Linguistics*, vol. IV, 246-248. New York/Oxford: Oxford University Press.
163. "General Linguistics and the Study of Morphological Processes". *Oceanic Linguistics* 31. 1-11.
164. "Pražské inspirace v mém jazykovědném myšlení". *Slovo a slovesnost* 53. 81-85. [Translation of the public address on the occasion of Prof. Uhlenbeck's doctorate honoris causa at Charles University of Prague, October 4, 1991: "Prague Inspiration in My Linguistic Thinking".]
165. "Antonymic Processes within the System of Javanese Adjectives". T. Dutton - M. Ross - D. Tryon (eds.), *The Language Game: Papers in Memory of Donald C. Laycock*, 491-500. Canberra: Australian National University. (Pacific Linguistics, series C-110)
166. "Some Critical Remarks on a Recent Interpretation of a Sentence from the Old Javanese Tantri Kamandaka". *Bijdragen tot de Taal-, Land- en Volkenkunde* 148. 262-269.
167. "Distinctions in the Study of Linguistic Semantics". A. Heen Wold (ed.), *The Dialogical Alternative. Towards a Theory of Language and Mind*, 273-291. Oslo: Scandinavian University Press.

1993

168. "De dreiging van snelle taalsterfte, een sinds kort onderkend mondiaal probleem". *Ons Erfdeel* 36. 23-31.
169. "The Threat of Rapid Language Death, a Recently Acknowledged Global Problem". *The Low Countries. Arts and society in Flanders and the Netherlands. A Yearbook, 1993-1994*, 25-31. Brugge: Stichting Ons Erfdeel.
170. R: *Talen zonder grenzen*. Verslag van een conferentie door de Verkenningscommissie Moderne Letteren op 23 oktober 1992. *Ons Erfdeel* 36. 786-788.

1994

171. "The Birth of NIAS". *22 1/2 Years of NIAS*, 15-24. Wassenaar: NIAS.
172. "De positie van woord en zin in taal en taalwetenschap". *Neerlandica extra muros* 32:2. 1-9.
173. "Functional Sentence Perspective in Modern and Old Javanese". S. Čmejrková - F. Štícha (eds.), *The Syntax of Sentence and Text. A Festschrift for František Daneš*, 179-192. Amsterdam/ Philadelphia: Benjamins.

1995

174. "Morphonology and Morphology: Two Systematic Aspects of Word Structure". W. Winter (ed.), *On Languages and Language. The Presidential Addresses of the 1991 Meeting of the Societas Linguistica Europaea*, 257-266. Berlin/New York: Mouton de Gruyter.

175. "Georges Mounin, 20 juni 1910-10 januari 1993". *Koninklijke Nederlandse Akademie van Wetenschappen: Levensberichten en herdenkingen 1994*, 81-86.

1996

176. "Some Remarks on Homonymy and Polysemy". B.H. Partee - P. Sgall (eds.), *Discourse and Meaning. Papers in Honor of Eva Hajičová*, 119-126. Amsterdam/Philadelphia: Benjamins.

177. "The Concepts of Process, Category, and Productivity in Morphology". V. Law - W. Hüllen (eds.), *Linguists and Their Diversions. A Festschrift for R.H. Robins on his 75th birthday*, 395-405. Münster: Nodus.

Forthcoming:

178. "Basic Concepts of Morphological Theory".
179. "Old Javanese Word Structure".
180. "About *cran-* and *cranberry*".

E.M. UHLENBECK

Javanese Linguistics,
A Retrospect and Some Prospects

JAVANESE LINGUISTICS,
A RETROSPECT AND SOME PROSPECTS*

I

Looking back upon the long period that I have been engaged in the study of Javanese, I have arrived at the conclusion that four guiding principles or rules have largely determined my course as a linguist. Let me take them up one by one and explore the consequences of their adoption.

First of all I have always felt that the key to the scientific study of a language which is not one's native tongue is a thorough command of that language. One has to learn to read, to listen and to speak, before one can hope to arrive at an understanding of the structure of a language. In this respect I owe a great deal to Balai Pustaka, the Bureau of Popular Literature in Batavia (now: Jakarta), where I spent a few most fruitful years under the expert and friendly guidance of the Javanese editors Koesrin, Poerwadarminta and Hardjawiraga. Six days a week, seven hours per day of either reading, speaking or listening to Javanese prepared me for the study of Javanese in an unparalleled way. It is this practical knowledge which gives access to the object to be studied scientifically. It gives access, but no more than that. Practical knowledge is a necessary but not a sufficient condition for doing linguistic research. It is not enough even for making the most simple observation. For that one needs a theory, that is, a consistent set of assumptions about the object to be studied. On this point I am indebted to Dr. Hidding, then head of Balai Pustaka, who understood the importance of this requirement better than most. It was he who acquainted me with the work of Pos, the outstanding Dutch linguist and philosopher, and this led me further into the general linguistic literature. I retain excellent memories of those few years in Batavia with days spent at Balai Pustaka in the study of Javanese followed by long, cool evenings in our garden, reading the classical works of Saussure, Sapir, Reichling, Bühler, Bloomfield, Cassirer, and luminaries of the previous century such as Paul, Wundt and von der Gabelentz. Although all I read was not easy for me to assimilate, it could not escape

* This paper is a slightly revised reprint of the valedictory address delivered in Leiden on May 31, 1983 on the occasion of the Fourth European Colloquium on Malay and Indonesian Studies, and published in the same year by the Koninklijk Instituut voor Taal-, Land- en Volkenkunde, which gave permission for this reprint.

me that an important transition in linguistics was taking place. The days
of an exclusive historical concern with language were over, and although
no general theory yet existed which could be used for descriptive pur-
poses, it was clear that the slowly emerging structural view of language
held great promise.

It only gradually dawned upon me what the consequences were of
taking seriously this requirement of defining one's theoretical position.
It began to demand a large share of my time and this has not changed
over the years. I did not and I do not deplore this. To the contrary, this
is in my opinion as it should be.

Closely related to this theoretical requirement is my conviction — and
this is then my third guiding principle — that one should be very cau-
tious in the use of concepts from traditional school-grammar for the
description of Indonesian languages and especially for their syntactic
description. This conviction was not born out of a careful analysis of
traditional grammar itself, but was based mainly on my experiences in
learning Javanese and Malay. From the very beginning I was so deeply
impressed by the deep-seated differences between these languages on
the one hand, and Greek and Latin on the other, the languages for the
description of which traditional grammar had originally been devised,
that I simply could not imagine that traditional grammar would be of
great use. Accordingly, I took the radical step in my Javanese grammar
of 1941 of breaking away completely from traditional syntactic concepts
such as subject, predicate and object. Instead I decided to make use of
sentence intonation as a means for distinguishing between a number of
basic sentence types. Ever since I have maintained my distrust of the ill-
defined conceptual framework of traditional grammar. I will not completely exclude the possibility that I have been too negative in this
respect, and that I have overlooked valuable elements in the traditional
categories, but I still believe that their uncritical wholesale acceptance,
because of their so-called intuitive relevance, is to be rejected, and I am
glad that I have not remained alone in this view.

A fourth characteristic of my way of doing linguistics is the amount of
attention given to the collection of data. Already at the time when I
worked on my book on Javanese morphophonemics I had noticed that
the existing Javanese grammatical treatises — and not only those! —
suffered from a seriously defective factual basis. I realized that it was
imperative for the discovery of the structure of a language to make
systematic and large-scale use of data from two basically different but
complementary sources: actual instances of the oral or written use of
language, and data elicited from native speakers. Both types of data have
their weak and strong points. By using both, one can reduce their weak-
nesses to a minimum. Instances of language use provide genuine material uninfluenced by the linguist, but they are quite accidental in relation

to the purpose of the linguist. Data from informants can be collected systematically, but here the linguist faces the very real danger of influencing his informant, so that he supplies the linguist with the data the linguist wants him to supply.

The decision to make use of informants has two consequences. In the first place it implies that one has to address oneself to the difficult question of the relationship of a speaker to his native language, and the appreciation by the linguist of his reflection on his language. Or, to use the dangerous terminology in vogue in generative grammar which faced the same problem, what is it that constitutes the speaker's competence or tacit knowledge of his language?

The answer to this question cannot be a uniform one. There is unanimity and divergence among the reactions of one's informants. This is to be expected because of the differences in attitude towards their language, and because of the nature of language in which obligatory and free aspects are combined. Unanimity among informants is more likely when questions are asked about what is obligatory, and divergence is normal when the linguist touches upon matters where freedom exists and creativity can make itself felt. It is for these two reasons that a plurality of informants should be employed by the linguist.

In the second place the use of informants forced me to pay attention to the interview situation itself, and this made me again leave the Indonesian area. Linguists are not the only ones who have to derive scientific information from contact with other people, and since within linguistics practically no work of any importance had been done on this question in the early fifties, I decided to take a look at other disciplines which could be expected to face comparable problems. It turned out that in particular Sullivan's study of the psychiatric interview (1954) helped me greatly in understanding the bilateral nature of the linguistic interview. It is not only the linguist who elicits information from the informant; the informant also derives information from the interviewer and this has to be taken into account by the linguist. Informants change under the impact of each interview. They often wonder about the questions being asked and sometimes they make up little theories of their own — often completely erroneous ones. The linguist should therefore guide this inevitable process of growing linguistic awareness in his informants by telling them the purpose of his questioning, so that they gradually develop from passive sources of information into valuable participants in the research of the linguist.

I also began to understand the importance of interviewing informants separately, in pleasant, unhurried conversations of limited duration, conducted in the target language. I found it necessary to employ them for several months or even for longer periods so that I could probe into questions already explored earlier. Only if one is very well acquainted with one's informants, and if one understands their position within the speech community and their attitude towards their language, is full evaluation of the data received possible.

II

To learn the language, to build a workable theoretical framework, to get rid of traditional conceptions and prejudices, and to establish a sound factual basis — these are the four objectives which in my opinion have to be attained if research is to bear fruit.

Let me, after these four "panchronic" characteristics, now look into the past from a diachronical angle.

It could hardly escape the attention of the student of general linguistics that this subject was and still is to the present day primarily based on the study of a very limited set of mostly Indo-European languages. Historically this is understandable. However, if linguistics really wanted to become a general science of language, it needed a much more diversified linguistic basis. To contribute to this goal by providing extensive data on the structure of Javanese was one of my earliest ambitions.

The course which I followed in working towards this goal has largely been determined by the general development of linguistics after Saussure, Sapir, and Bloomfield. Like many other linguists who responded to the call for a synchronic and functional description, I began with that part of language that had proved itself most amenable to a structural description, that is with the study of the phonemic system, before moving to the study of morphology, and still later to syntax. In my case I was very soon deeply impressed by the Prague school. I vividly remember the time when I became acquainted with that school through a badly stencilled, hardly legible copy of van Wijk's "Phonology, a chapter of structural linguistics", purchased in 1941 from Dr. Swellengrebel for the price of one *ringgit*. It is in my book on the structure of the Javanese morpheme that the influence of three of the most conspicuous members of the Prague school, Mathesius, Trubetzkoy, and Jakobson, is clearly visible.

Apart from its contribution to the description of Modern Javanese, this monograph, which was my first larger study in Javanese linguistics, has some features which deserve to be mentioned briefly here, as they are of more general interest. These are the following: (1) the use made of quantitative data as a means of discovering qualitative morphonological regularities which otherwise would have escaped one's attention; (2) the application of the distinction between the centre and the periphery of language structure; and (3) the value of the distinction between absolute, exceptionless rules and statistical rules which permit exceptions.

Perhaps I should add that within Indonesian linguistics as a whole the monograph was rather unusual not only because of its subject-matter, but also because of its intimate relation with general linguistics. As such it is an early example of a type of work which now has become much more common.

As I have already said, the shift from phonology to the study of morphology was a natural one. I just followed a general trend. The future task of structural linguistics was clear. It faced a task of extrapolation. There was general agreement that the principles underlying phonology, which had proved to be so fruitful in that area, had a wider validity, and therefore could also be applied to other domains of language structure. Jakobson, with his well-known morphology articles of the early thirties, had shown the way. Much later A.W. de Groot in this country did the same for syntax.

For me, however, there was an additional, quite different — more down to earth — motive for occupying myself as soon as possible with morphology. Early in January 1950 I took over from C.C. Berg the Leiden Chair of Javanese, and this meant that I had to take over directly after the Christmas vacation the sixteen hours of instruction my indefatigable predecessor used to give. This led to a number of rather humiliating experiences, as I was unable to give satisfactory answers to what seemed simple and sensible morphological questions from my students. Why is it that for instance in one case a verb form with the suffix -ake has this meaning, and in an other case a quite different one? And what about the duplicated forms which occurred in such bewildering variety, or the forms with suffix -an, or what about the verb forms with prefix ka- or kĕ-? On the basis of my practical knowledge, sometimes assisted by information from the Gericke - Roorda and Pigeaud dictionaries, I was usually able to determine the meaning of each form in its particular context, but I nevertheless felt highly uncomfortable. There must be regularity and therefore there must be statable rules, but I did not know them. In short: I had only the vaguest ideas about what made Javanese morphology really tick.

It was obvious that this state of ignorance had to be remedied as soon as possible. In harmony with my basic rules mentioned earlier, I had first to develop a theoretical basis for my morphological research. This implied in the first place that I had to evaluate both Berg's monograph on the Javanese verb published in 1937 as volume 95 of the *Bijdragen* and the negative review of his work by Gonda in the same journal, and of course also Gonda's article in the *Bijdragen* on the word-classes in Indonesian. Secondly I had to come to terms with recent developments in the United States.

My article on the study of word-classes in Javanese, published in *Lingua* in 1953, contained the first results of my theoretical reflections on Javanese morphology. In spite of the at that time prestigious position in linguistics of the Neo-Bloomfieldians, I arrived at the conclusion that their asemantic morphemics had to be rejected. In a paper delivered at the summer meeting of the Linguistic Society of America held in Bloomington, Indiana in the same year, I explained — as I recall, not without trepidation — why this approach which pays attention only to forms and their distribution, held no attraction for me. The main reason was that I had become convinced, following Jakobson and the Prague school and the Amsterdam group of structuralists, that linguistics is concerned with data which owe their very existence to the simultaneous presence of both sound and meaning. Moreover, I had experienced myself in my study of Javanese the essential correctness of Reichling's views concerning the word as the central unit of language and language use, fundamentally different, especially because of its syntactic and semantic properties, from the morpheme.

As I held the view that morphology is the study of synchronic processes in which both form and meaning are involved, to be described from a structural point of view, that is with full use of the concepts of opposition and complementary distribution, I could accept neither Berg's nor Gonda's approach. Moreover, the factual basis of Berg's monograph was so limited — it rested mainly on the Gericke - Roorda dictionary — that I decided that I had to make a fresh start. This was for me a painful conclusion, but an inevitable one as it rested in my opinion on sound arguments. I was now also forced to take a closer look at semantics and especially at word meaning and its relation to so-called grammatical meaning. I was fortunate in those years to have the benefit of frequent contact with Pos, Reichling, and De Groot. Particularly valuable were the long, unforgettable discussions with De Groot in Aerdenhout, and especially with Pos in Haarlem which only came to an end when the last bus to Voorhout was already moving. His death in September 1955 was a serious blow.

It goes without saying that again according to my maxims I began to collect a great mass of material, and it was an interesting experience that simply in this way some discoveries could be made. Let me give one example. It was of course known from Roorda's grammar onwards that there existed a so-called accidental passive in Javanese, but apparently nobody had bothered to find out according to what procédé this passive was formed, although it must have been clear to anyone that if there was such a productive category, the speakers of the language — one way or other — must have mastered this procédé. In other words: there must be a rule. As a matter of fact this rule could easily be discovered: *kĕ*- is prefixed before stems beginning with a consonant, *k*- before stems beginning with a vowel. When this became clear, it was not difficult to determine the relation of this accidental passive to the *ka*-, *-in*-, and *di*-passives, and order became visible out of a previously chaotic situation. In general systematic investigation of form-meaning relationships between words with due attention to the concept of proportionality turned out to be of central importance.

For the study of open systems such as nouns, verbs, and adjectives, the concepts of productivity and potentiality proved to be equally indispensable. Over the years I began to understand that in morphology one needs an approach which is partly entitative and partly processual. This view stands midway between the Neo-Bloomfieldian one which was completely entitative, and the view of Chomsky and his followers who had only an eye for the processual aspect. In general I have been attracted more to middle-of-the-road positions than to extreme ones. This also pertains to larger linguistic issues, such as the position of linguistics as a discipline which has a psychological as well as a sociological aspect, but which in my opinion is part neither of psychology nor of sociology.

As to Javanese morphology it appeared that one of the most striking characteristics, which it certainly shares with Sundanese and other West-Indonesian languages, is that the same formal means are used over and over again, not only in different morphological subsystems, but also in syntax and in the lexicon. A very clear illustration is duplication which could be shown to play different roles, first of all in various word classes, but also in the lexicon, in syntax, and even in morphonology. My succinct structural analysis of the various duplication and reduplication phenomena within one single language, which stand in a sharp contrast with Gonda's earlier comparative treatment in *Lingua* of the same phenomena, is perhaps the most illustrative example of my early work on morphology.

It is obvious that morphology is intimately related to lexicology, the former being concerned with the systematic aspects of the vocabulary, the latter with its idiosyncratic features. My study of the noun *rasa*, 'taste, feeling, deepest meaning, essence', and its derivates, written to bring out the contrast with Berg's earlier discussion of *krasa* in his *Bijdragen* monograph, also tried to show that new insights into morphological relations would have consequences for the form and content of many lemmata of the dictionary.

In conclusion one may say that a number of morphological regularities have been discovered and that in broad outline the structure of Javanese morphology as a whole has become visible. It also became clear that Javanese morphology was much more complicated than one previously had tended to assume because of its small number of formally different affixes.

This is not to say that my studies in Javanese morphology have led to anything like a full description. They are mostly *Vorarbeiten*, explorations into an area which is still largely unknown territory. Only two closed systems, the pronominal system and the numerals, have been described in such detail that they may be viewed as chapters of a future Javanese grammar. I particularly regret that I have not yet been able to do what I announced as early as 1956 in my contribution to the first Jakobson Festschrift: to publish the supporting data for the partial description of the Javanese verb system given in that article. Especially the data which pertain to the semantic differences between the suffixless verbs, the verbs with suffix -i, and the suffix -ake, would be valuable both for our morphological and for our lexicological knowledge. Moreover, they may form the basis for research into the syntax of verbal word groups, and this includes the difficult problem of the auxiliaries to which I have given much attention in the recent past. There are several other serious lacunae in my morphological work. Although data have been collected, my study of conjunctions, interjections, prepositions, modal elements such as *koq*, *raq*, *jĕbul*, and *dadaq* with very restricted or even zero morphological valence, has not progressed far enough for its results to be published.

In view of the importance I have always attached to theory as an instrument for research, it is not surprising that the advent of transformational grammar heralded in 1957 by Chomsky's *Syntactic Structures* could not be ignored. The claim made by Chomsky in his *Aspects of the Theory of Syntax* of 1965 and in later publications were so fundamental and far-reaching, and held such serious and unpleasant consequences for all those who had been working within a different theoretical paradigm — to use the popular formula — that it was imperative to arrive at a fair, unbiased appraisal of the new approach and its deeper implications.

Much was at stake. If Chomsky and the rapidly growing number of his followers were right, there was only one course to follow: to abandon my theoretical views, to adopt the new ways of linguistic thinking and to apply them to the Javanese facts. This was the second time that I had to face and to evaluate a new and persuasive, strongly dogmatic movement within general linguistics: first the Neo-Bloomfieldians and now their at first sight radically different successors, who especially till about 1970 were utterly convinced of their superiority, as they felt they had succeeded in making linguistics into a real science, which meant in this view a science similar to the natural sciences.

For me a long period of theoretical reflection began, a period which I consider the most crucial one in my career as a linguist. It was clear that if changes in my theoretical position had to be made, these would have to be radical. To mention just a few points. Till 1972 generative grammar hardly recognized morphology as a component of language structure distinct from syntax and phonology. At least till 1976 no generative grammarian attached any value to the word as a central unit of language, and in general to the concept of the linguistic sign, so essential for those who worked in a tradition inspired by Saussure. Generative grammar attempted to describe a language by means of a closed system of rules, while I had gradually begun to appreciate that language functions in close cooperation with extra-linguistic information. And there were other issues on which our respective views were almost diametrically opposed, like for instance about the centrality of syntax, the distinction between semantics and pragmatics, and the autonomy of linguistics (see Uhlenbeck 1978b, 1983).

There was another motive for turning to or rather concentrating on general linguistic theory. From 1958 onwards, the year in which I was appointed to the Chair of General Linguistics, I was faced with the task of presenting to a growing number of students a general introduction to linguistic theory. This meant that the days of unhurried, piecemeal and gradual development of theoretical instruments for the description of Javanese were over. Now I had to make a serious effort to tie together my views on phonology, morphology, semantics, and syntax into a consistent and coherent whole which could be presented as a viable alternative to transformational generative grammar. In retrospect, I believe that the pressure exerted by the latter theory was for me very beneficial. It forced me to address myself to a number of issues which otherwise had perhaps not caught my attention. They were mainly related to syntax and semantics, as it was those provinces of linguistic structure on which the theoretical discussion began to focus, especially since it was generally recognized in the mid-sixties, also in transformational generative circles, that semantics was part and parcel of linguistics.

As could be expected, my work on Javanese was delayed by this occupation with general issues, but it did not entirely come to a stop. I continued my studies in Javanese morphology with a certain preference for those more or less marginal domains which had previously received little descriptive attention, although they were of interest not only for general linguistics, but in some cases for other disciplines as well. Examples are the proper names, subject of much discussion among philosophers such as Russell and Wittgenstein, and kinship terminology, a central topic in anthropology.

However, more effort went into syntax, in accordance with the general line of extrapolation mentioned earlier.

Following the same pattern as in morphology, I first tried to build a basis for my descriptive efforts in this new area, being convinced that my earlier prewar work lacked a solid theoretical foundation. After some general articles published between 1958 and 1964 which take up a position comparable to my article on word classes of 1953, I felt that I was sufficiently prepared to take up the study of nominal and verbal groups in Javanese. A *Lingua* article published in 1965 contained some preliminary results. Upon further reflection, however, I became convinced that my conception of syntax was still deficient. Its scope was too narrow, as it concentrated on word grouping, but neglected the structure of the sentence taken as a whole. Moreover, it did not accord to the intonational phenomena the place which they should occupy. This onesidedness was remedied by the introduction of the concept of sentence segmentation, a phenomenon which, as Bally had shown, plays an important role in French. The concept of sentence segment proved to be useful for a better understanding of the topic-comment mechanism and more generally of the way obligatory and non-obligatory aspects of syntax function together. A brief account of my present views on syntax is found in my "Sentence Segment and Word Group, Basic Concepts of Javanese Syntax", published in 1975. It is this conception of syntax which has been applied in my recent reexamination of the various constructions with *sing* or *kang* and *oleh* or *ěnggone*, and also in my research on topic and focus constructions in Old Javanese. It even proved a useful concept for my efforts to interpret the Old Javanese Rāmāyaṇa-kakawin.

Recognition of the quite different functions fulfilled by word grouping and by sentence segmentation confirmed the need to distinguish between strict rules indispensable for the description of obligatory phenomena, and rules of preference and avoidance which are equally indispensable when there is a certain freedom of choice. In general it helped me to understand better the relation between syntax and semantics. In contrast to the traditional Chomskyan view which has always afforded a central position to syntax, I became more and more convinced of the converse: in relation to semantics, syntax fulfills essentially only an ancillary role. For this reason and probably also in reaction to other quite different views on meaning, I considered it necessary to pay attention again to what one may call the semantic instruments which every speaker has at his disposal, and in general to define my position in semantics by making it more articulate. This resulted in my "Semantics from a Linguistic Perspective", published in 1981.

It is clear that having arrived at this point in time, I am very close to the end of my brief look into my linguistic past.

From the point of view of Javanese the results of my intermittent efforts have been modest. My old ambitious project to furnish a description as exhaustive as possible of Modern Javanese has not been accomplished. The things that still have to be done outnumber and outweigh what has been achieved, and the results of what has been achieved are of course far from definite. There are, however, two consoling thoughts, a general and a specific one. The general consideration from which I may derive some comfort is that the study of language has expanded so much that a full description of one language has become an entreprise which exceeds the powers of a single person, as is proved by the results of the study of Modern English in which so many scholars are still engaged. The specific consolation is that my descriptive work related to most subsystems of Javanese offers enough stimuli for others to take over where I have left off.

III

And now the final item on my agenda: the prospects for Javanese linguistic studies.

Let us first take a very brief look at the object of these studies, that is at the Javanese language itself. The first thing to notice is that the social position of the language has undergone an important change.

Up to the Japanese occupation of Java in March 1942, Javanese as used by educated Javanese in Surakarta was — be it slowly — developing into some sort of standard language. It had the official approval of the Dutch colonial government and it had a certain cultural prestige. It was similar, if not identical, to the Javanese used in the schoolbooks disseminated by the Department of Education in Batavia and by the local authorities in Central and East Java, to the Javanese used in journals and weeklies such as *Sedyatama*, *Darmakanḍa*, and *Penyebar Semangat*, or to the Javanese of the manifold publications emanating from Balai Pustaka.

Although Javanese had been influenced by Malay for a very long time, Indonesian had remained for most Javanese a foreign language. Speeches in Indonesian delivered at Javanese meetings by people from Minangkabau or other areas of Sumatra proved to be difficult to understand for most people in the audience.

Upon closer observation, however, it appeared that the position of Javanese was less secure. It had an Achilles' heel: it was considered not to be a suitable medium for discussing modern political and cultural issues and ideas. Only Indonesian could function as such. This was reflected in the Javanese literature. Except for some short stories, there was very little in what was written in Javanese which found inspiration in problems of modern Indonesian society.

Already during the war period, and increasingly so after Indonesia became independent, the influence of Indonesian grew. It was on its way to becoming the national language. It took over the position of Dutch at all levels of government administration. It was rapidly introduced into the educational system as the language of instruction in all schools and universities. A process of osmosis, of mutual interpenetration of the two languages, was set in motion, and this is still in progress. Large-scale lexical borrowing took place and certainly also morphological and syntactic borrowing, but what seems more important is that the communicative functions fulfilled by Javanese have become quite limited. At present it is only within the family circle and among friends that Javanese is still regularly used, and this only if the topic of conversation does not preclude this. Nowadays, many aspects of modern life can be more readily discussed in Indonesian than in Javanese. To what extent this account is true for the rural population is still unknown.

What are the consequences of this change in the object of study for the prospects of Javanese linguistics? I believe that in the present situation language variation and multilingualism seem to be natural objects of study. Java has become one of the most attractive fields for doing sociolinguistic research. This research has to be conducted in the field by researchers who are equally at home in Javanese and in Indonesian, or, if the area is East Java, certainly also in Madurese, while some knowledge of Dutch and English is certainly not a luxury.

The data recently published by Suseno Kartomihardjo on communicative codes in East Java may be seen as a first move into this largely unexplored territory. Even traditional dialect studies have rarely been made. I do not have to add after what I have said about my own work, that here again results may be expected only if full use is made of the methods developed in sociolinguistics, which so rapidly became of age after Labov's dissertation of 1966. Moreover, a strong exemplary influence may be exerted in the near future by Grijns' eagerly awaited monograph on the language situation of Jakarta (Grijns 1991).

My plea for sociolinguistic research should, however, not be misunderstood. It does not imply that one could forego a structural analysis. The danger of a too exclusive concentration on social and dialectal language variation is that it easily acquires an anecdotal character. The study of language variation is a necessary corrective and refinement of structural analysis which often operated on the far too simple assumption that all speakers of a language have the same relation to their language, regardless of their position in society. The more Java develops into a multilingual society, the more this becomes unacceptable.

References

BALLY, Ch. 1932 [1944²]. *Linguistique générale et linguistique française*. Berne: Francke. [440 pp.]

BERG, C.C. 1937. *Bijdrage tot de kennis der Javaansche werkwoordsvormen. BKI (= Bijdragen tot de Taal-, Land- en Volkenkunde)* 95. [396 pp.]

GERICKE, J.F.C. – ROORDA, T. 1901[4]. *Javaansch - Nederlandsch Woordenboek*. Amsterdam/Leiden: Müller/Brill. [2 vols.; xii + 905 + 872 pp.]

GONDA, J. 1949. "Prolegomena tot een theorie der woordsoorten in Indonesische talen". *BKI* 105. 275-331.

—. 1949. "Over Indonesische werkwoordsvormen". *BKI* 105. 333-379, 381-421.

—. 1950. "The Functions of Word Duplication in Indonesian Languages". *Lingua* 2. 170-197.

GRIJNS, C.D. 1991. *Jakarta Malay*. 2 vols. Leiden: KITLV [2 vols.; xx + 292 + vi + 156 pp.]

DE GROOT, A.W. 1949. *Structurele syntaxis*. Den Haag: Servire. [289 pp.]

JAKOBSON, R. 1932. "Zur Struktur des russischen Verbums". *Charisteria Guilelmo Mathesio quinquagenario oblata*, 74-84. Prague.

—. 1936. "Beitrag zur allgemeinen Kasuslehre. Gesamtbedeutung der russischen Kasus". *Travaux du Cercle linguistique de Prague* 6. 240-288.

LABOV, W. 1966. *The Social Stratification of English in New York City*. Washington D.C.: Center for Applied Linguistics. [xii + 655 pp.]

PIGEAUD, Th. 1938. *Javaans - Nederlands Handwoordenboek*. Groningen/Batavia. [xii + 624 pp.]

POS, H.J. 1938. "Phonologie en betekenisleer". *Mededeelingen der Koninklijke Nederlandsche Akademie van Wetenschappen, Afd. Letterkunde*, N.S. deel 1, 577-600.

—. 1939. "Perspectives du structuralisme". *Travaux du Cercle linguistique de Prague* 8. 71-78.

—. 1939. "Phénoménologie et linguistique". *Revue Internationale de Philosophie* 1. 354-365.

SULLIVAN, H. Stack. 1954. *The Psychiatric Interview*. New York: Norton. [xxiii + 246 pp.]

SUSENO KARTOMIHARDJO. 1981. *Ethnography of Communicative Codes in East Java*. Pacific Linguistics Series D no 39. [xi + 212 pp.]

ROORDA, T. 1855. *Javaansche grammatica*. Amsterdam.

UHLENBECK, E.M. 1941. "Interessante vertalingen". *Tijdschrift van het Koninklijk Bataviaasch Genootschap van Kunsten en Wetenschappen* 81. 295-306.

—. 1941. *Beknopte Javaansche grammatica*. Batavia: Volkslectuur. [107 pp.]

—. 1953a. "The Study of Word Classes in Javanese". *Lingua* 3. 322-354.

—. 1953b. "Woordverdubbeling in het Javaans". *Bijdragen tot de Taal-, Land- en Volkenkunde* 109. 52-61.

—. 1956. "Verb Structure in Javanese". *For Roman Jakobson. Essays on the occasion of his sixtieth birthday*, 567-573. The Hague: Mouton.

50   E.M. UHLENBECK

—. 1958. "Traditionele zinsontleding en syntaxis". *Levende Talen* 193. 18-30.
—. 1959. "Die mit javanisch *rasa* morphologisch zusammenhängenden Wörter. Ein Beitrag zur javanischen Lexikologie". *Oriens Extremus* 6. 104-115.
—. 1962. "De beginselen van het syntactisch onderzoek". In: A.J.B.N. REICHLING e.a., *Taalonderzoek in onze tijd*, 17-37. Den Haag: Servire.
—. 1964. "Betekenis en syntaxis". *Forum der Letteren* 5. 67-82.
—. 1965. "Some Preliminary Remarks on Javanese Syntax". *Lingua* 15. 53-70.
—. 1975. "Sentence Segment and Word Group, Basic Concepts of Javanese Syntax". In: J.W.M. VERHAAR ed. *Miscellaneous Studies in Indonesian and Languages in Indonesia*, vol. 1. 6-10. Jakarta: Badan Penyelenggara Seri NUSA.
—. 1978a. *Studies in Javanese Morphology*. (Koninklijk Instituut voor Taal-, Land- en Volkenkunde, Translation series 19). The Hague: Nijhoff. [vi + 361 pp.]
—. 1978b. "On the Distinction between Linguistics and Pragmatics". In: David GERVER - H.Wallace SINAIKO eds., *Language Interpretation and Communication*, 185-198. New York/London: Plenum.
—. 1981. "Betekenis in linguïstisch perspectief". *Mededelingen der Kon. Ned. Akademie van Wetenschappen, Afd. Letterkunde*, N.S. deel 44:8. 339-360.
—. 1983. *Linguistics: Neither Psychology nor Sociology*. [= Uhlenbeck-Lecture 1]. Wassenaar: NIAS. [24 pp.]
VAN WIJK, N. 1939. *Phonologie. Een hoofdstuk uit de structurele taalwetenschap*. Den Haag: Nijhoff. [xiv + 207 pp.]
ZOETMULDER, P.J. 1982. *Old Javanese - English Dictionary*. The Hague. [2 vols.; 2368 pp.]

TABLE OF CONTENTS